Story Times Good Enough to Eat!

Story Times Good Enough to Eat!

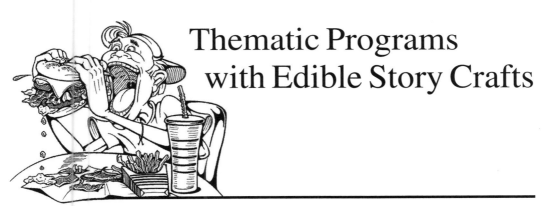

Thematic Programs with Edible Story Crafts

Melissa Rossetti Folini

LIBRARIES UNLIMITED

AN IMPRINT OF ABC-CLIO, LLC
Santa Barbara, California • Denver, Colorado • Oxford, England

Library of Congress Cataloging-in-Publication Data
Folini, Melissa Rossetti.
   Story times good enough to eat! : thematic programs with edible story crafts / Melissa Rossetti Folini.
      p. cm.
   Includes bibliographical references and index.
   ISBN 978-1-59158-898-6 (pbk. : alk. paper) — ISBN 978-1-59158-899-3 (ebook) 1. Cookery. 2. Handicraft. 3. Children's stories. 4. Creative activities and seat work. I. Title.
TX714.F646   2010
641.5—dc22   2009049894

ISBN: 978-1-59158-898-6
EISBN: 978-1-59158-899-3

14 13 12 11 10   1 2 3 4 5

This book is also available on the World Wide Web as an eBook.
Visit www.abc-clio.com for details.

ABC-CLIO, LLC
130 Cremona Drive, P.O. Box 1911
Santa Barbara, California 93116-1911

This book is printed on acid-free paper ∞
Manufactured in the United States of America

I would like to dedicate this book to all the children who attended story times over the years at the Chester Public Library. This book came about because of you and your eager participation!

It is dedicated to all the staff I had over the years for willingly implementing whatever crazy idea I came up with.

It is also dedicated to Mimi for encouragement and to Rocky for belief and support and a change in Labor Day plans. What a difference a year makes.

Contents

Introduction

Say good-bye to boring story times with the same books and obligatory graham cracker and apple juice snack. Say hello to fun themes, books designed to keep children from getting bored, and an edible craft they will remember long after the crumbs have been cleaned up.

This manual is intended to help busy librarians, teachers, and child care providers run successful, creative, and memorable story times. These programs not only keep the children engaged, but take minimal time to plan, are cost effective, and offer you a unique time-saving way to introduce children to the magical world of books and reading.

The ideas and themes presented in this book use food use as a creative craft/snack and can be easily implemented no matter what the setting or time frame allotted for the activity. There is no paint to dry or glue to set; and children make not only their craft, but also their snack—all at the same time!

Program Guidelines

These thematic story times are geared for children between three and eight years old. However, they are simple enough to be adapted for children as young as two and can also be engaging for children up to the age of ten. The younger children may require a bit of assistance from your staff, their guardians/parents, or perhaps another child who is a bit older. The idea is for them to have fun making their craft/snack. Keep in mind that the finished product does not have to look exactly like the pictures in this book or be perfect for youngsters to participate in and enjoy the experience.

For each story time, read two or three of the theme-related stories to the children. Suggested reading lists have been provided with each theme. Then describe to the children the edible craft they are about to make. Specific instructions are provided for making the craft. Because these crafts are edible, once they are done, allow the children to eat them. Serve juice or other beverages if you wish, or the children may take their creations home to eat later.

During my tenure as library director at the Chester Public Library, a small rural library in New Hampshire, I used these activities with great success, and I have used most of the books listed. The books have been chosen for their wording and illustrations; and many have rhyming text, which helps keep the children interested and engaged, while building literacy skills!

Ingredients/Materials and Instructions

This manual was designed with the idea that as long as you have a few staple supplies on hand, you will be able to present most of these programs in a very short amount of time with minimal impact on your budget. The chapters are based on individual themes. For each theme you'll find a booklist of stories to read aloud to the children, along with a recipe and instructions on how to make the edible craft after the stories have been read.

The number of ingredients and amount of material needed will vary, depending on the number of children who participate in your program, so be sure to adjust your amounts accordingly.

The beauty of these recipes is that many use the same ingredients; therefore, you can buy them in bulk at a better price and save some money and keep them on hand.

Basic Supplies Needed

- Beverage or cocktail napkins: At least one per child to set the craft on, and extra for "spills." If you use dessert-sized plates for the craft, you will only need to give the children a napkin to wipe their hands.

- Dessert-sized paper plates: These may be used in place of the cocktail napkins for children to set their crafts on. You will need one per child.

- Six- to eight-ounce paper/plastic juice cups: These are used for measuring portions, as well as for beverages if you choose to serve them, so you may need up to three per child per craft.

- Plastic knives: Have one per child per craft on hand.

- Styrofoam or plastic bowls: Use these to measure portions, or fill them and place them "family-style" in the center of the worktable. You should have one bowl for every five children, for them to share.

- Food coloring in assorted colors: A little goes a long way, and one box of assorted colors should last you quite a while.

- Several 15-ounce tubs of white and chocolate premade icing. These keep for quite some time if they are unopened. So if you see a sale, stock up!

From *Story Times Good Enough to Eat!: Thematic Programs with Edible Story Crafts* by Melissa Rossetti Folini. Santa Barbara, CA: Libraries Unlimited. Copyright © 2010.

Note: For the recipes that use icing, it is better to divide it into portions before the story time using plastic cups and give each child his or her own plastic knife. The instructions for each program assume that the icing has already been divided up.

A word about beverages: it is up to you whether to add a beverage to these programs; you may not have the budget or the setting to do so. If you wish to add beverages to the program, it is best stick with a clear juice, milk, or even water to avoid allergic reactions and nasty stains on the carpet. White grape juice is a great alternative to apple juice. In my experience, many children are either tired of apple juice or just don't like it, so a lot gets thrown away. White grape juice is available in most major grocery stores. It is a clear juice, so there will be no dark red or purple stains if any is spilled. Milk is a good complement to those recipes that call for frosting, cookies, or peanut butter, but it can be pricey. Water is an inexpensive and easy to clean solution. If you serve a beverage, you may use the same cups you already have on hand for use with the frosting, measuring out portions, etc. Again, these are simply suggestions.

Safety

Although the utensils recommended for these recipes are plastic, there is always the chance of injury. Please remind children not to lick the knives or put them in their mouths, as they are sharp and could cause a cut or scrape. Likewise, for any recipe in which an inedible material is included, carefully and clearly instruct the children to eat only the part that is food—not the cup, ribbon, string, and so forth. For recipes that contain inedible items, notations have been made as reminders.

Also make sure to refrigerate any baked goods that you are not using immediately, and any remaining jellies or frostings that have been opened. Seal up cereal, chips, and candy bags with tape, clips, or rubber bands to keep them fresh, especially if you will need them in a day or two for another program.

Food allergies are covered later on page xv.

Pre-Story Time Preparations

Theme/Book Selection

Preparing for the story time can help things go smoothly for you and the children. Some preparations should be done well in advance, whereas others may be done shortly before the program begins.

First, decide on the theme of your program. This can be done days, weeks, or even months ahead. If you choose a holiday, you will know many months ahead of time what you will need to execute that program. If you are presenting a theme such as animals, choose the day to present it as far in advance as possible.

Once you have chosen a theme, make sure you either have or can acquire the appropriate books. In many cases, your library will either have them or be able to obtain them through interlibrary loan or a reciprocal borrowing program. Of course, if you know you will use these programs repeatedly, it may be wise to invest in some of the books ahead of time, so you will

---

always have them ready for your programs. If you are on a budget, there are several online sites, such as eBay or Half.com, that sell used books at a considerable discount. You might also try your local Goodwill, Salvation Army, or other thrift store; they often carry huge selections of used books at very reasonable prices.

If you don't work in a library, ask local public or school librarians if their institutions allow educators or their patrons to place orders for discounted books with them. Each library has its own policy about this, and this may not be an option, but it doesn't hurt to ask. Often they will be willing to help in some way with anything that promotes reading and literacy in the community. Some of the parents of your children may already have these books in their own collections, and they might be willing to donate them. Send out a list of the titles you are looking for and ask the parents to check their collections to see if they have any of them. In some cases, a parent may even go out and buy the books for you outright as a donation. Most people are willing or even eager to help out in some way; you just need to tell them what your needs are.

Once you have chosen and obtained your books, put them on display if you have the space, as an advertisement of the upcoming program. If you like, add some coloring sheets on a small display table. This will help generate interest and work as a silent advertisement for you. Copy them from coloring books you already have or download them from the many online sites that offer free coloring pages for you to print and copy. If you type in "free coloring pages" in your search engine start page, you will find many options. Coloring sheets are an inexpensive activity and advertisement that can enhance any children's program.

A note of caution: If you're a librarian, make sure that the books you will be reading aren't checked out prior to your program; or if you are a teacher or child care provider, that they aren't taken home. To prevent this from happening, you may simply put a note on each books that says "for display only" until after the program, or display other theme-related books, holding back the ones you will actually be reading from.

Reader Selection

Another step in your planning is to decide who will be reading the stories. If you want to oversee the craft setup or have other duties to perform during the actual program, designate another staff member to read. You could also utilize a trusted volunteer or a reliable parent whom you know will be attending the program. Keep in mind that it is important to have a good reader. The person should be animated while reading the stories, to engage the children. The reader must also be reliable and punctual. Instruct the person to read over the books ahead of time, as many of them have tricky rhymes (which are part of the fun), and some may even contain words not always easy to pronounce! If the reader will be someone other than a staff member, be clear about your overall expectations and what time you want the reader to arrive.

Supply Inventory

After you have chosen the theme, acquired your books, and selected a reader, it's time to make sure you have the necessary ingredients and materials to make your edible craft. If you have already purchased the staple supplies and have them on hand, you will be in very good shape to put on your program. If not, make the necessary purchases.

If your setting allows, you may want to issue an announcement for the story time, with a sign-up sheet, so you will know how many cupcakes, cookies, etc., you need for the program. If you are in a school or day-care setting, you will already have your count of students. If you are unsure how many to plan for, keep in mind that it is always better to have too much than to run out. Sometimes older children and parents attend these programs, and they may help themselves to more than one snack, unaware that you had them carefully counted out. So it is always wise to have a few extras on hand. They won't go to waste, as any leftovers can be eaten by staff or taken home by your young attendees, who may want to take home something for their big brother or sister who wasn't able to come.

If the number of attendees is unknown, take an average of your usual program attendance and go with that. Most cupcake recipes will make at least a dozen, and packages of cookies easily contain more than 20. Once you have put on these programs a few times, you will have a better idea what you will need for your group. As previously mentioned, many of the ingredients are used in several different recipes, so in most cases you will be able to purchase one bag or box, seal it up, and save it for a different program, saving you both time and money.

The main key to keeping these programs simple is to prepare as much ahead of time as you can, so once you have decided on your theme and have your books, display, and head count, prepare your ingredients. The day of program will thus require minimal involvement on your part.

If your chosen craft has colored frosting, tint it the night before, so the color sets up. The longer it sits, the darker the color will become. You may also measure out portions of the frosting a day or a few hours ahead of time, cover the cups with plastic wrap, and put them in the fridge. Just remember to take them out an hour or so before story time so they soften to a spreadable consistency.

Before the children arrive, spread out your disposable plastic tablecloth, if you are using one, on whatever surface you will be using, and set out the napkins, plates, or plastic knives. Any "community" bowls of sprinkles, bits, etc., may also be placed in the center of your table for easy sharing. As soon as the story program is over, each child may go and sit or stand in front of his or her craft.

If you have a child-sized table, the children will be more comfortable sitting around it in chairs while creating their crafts. However if you are using a folding banquet table or reference table that is a bit higher, it is much easier to have the children stand around the table. They will be able to reach better, and without chairs you will be able to fit more children around the table. If you are short on elbow room, encourage the children to move away from the immediate area once they are finished.

If you have chosen a craft that involves cupcakes, you have a few options for acquiring them. You may purchase a mix and bake them yourself or have a staff member do so, or buy them premade. Cupcake liners are optional. They will make handling the cupcakes easier for the children and are often available in theme-appropriate designs and colors. However, they are not necessary, and they will be one of the first items the children discard when they have finished decorating their cupcakes.

You may also ask for volunteer help from a parent or guardian. Often parents are more than willing to help with programs and provide snacks; they are simply waiting to be asked. If you have a few reliable parents or volunteers, ask them to donate cupcakes; if you already have a mix, you could give it to them to make; or put out a sign-up sheet listing the programs you have coming up and specifying your material/ingredient needs.

A word of caution about having other people make these items for you: be VERY SPECIFIC about what you need. For example, explain that you need 12 UNFROSTED, vanilla cupcakes with specific liners or none at all, and that they should be a standard size. If you do not specify, you may end up with 24 mini chocolate cupcakes with frosting on them, or some other variation. People are willing to help, but they need direction. Also, be very clear about when you need the supplies. Do you want them the day before so you can check them over, or is it acceptable for your helpers to bring them to the program when they come? Volunteer help is a great resource as long as everyone is clear about exactly what they need to do.

Likewise, if parents or guardians accompany their children to the program, as is often the case in a public library, insist that they stay for the entire program, as staff have other duties and cannot be babysitting. Adults in attendance may assist their children in making their crafts, especially if the children are a bit younger. While you have the extra hands available, it never hurts to ask for help with cleanup. More than likely a few will volunteer, but don't be afraid to ask for assistance with trash or other tasks.

Finally, if time permits, make a "template" of your edible craft prior to story time so that children can see firsthand what they will be making. This will also give you a chance to figure out how best to instruct the children when they make their own, and you will be able to gauge how long it should take them to finish. At the end of the program it gets to be YOUR snack; enjoy!

After the Program

Depending on which program you present, your cleanup should take no more than 10 to 15 minutes. If you have portioned out the frosting in individual cups, discard them as soon as each child is done. You may also put away or discard any other item the children have used and are finished with. Be sure to explain that you are not rushing them, but rather making room for them to finish creating. This also removes the temptation of children or parents of consuming your leftovers/extra supplies simply because they are sitting there. Out of sight, out of mind. It also helps your cleanup go that much faster.

If you are not reusing any of the items that were on the table, it is best to discard any frosting your participants dipped into, along with any items that were in community bowls, as there is always the chance there was excess touching, or perhaps something was "sampled" and then returned to the bowl. For sanitary reasons, just discard these items. If you have used a disposable tablecloth, discard that as well, or sponge off and disinfect the table or tablecloth after all the children are done.

Tie up any trash bags and remove them from the room, or ask a volunteer to do so. This helps you avoid insect problems or odors from having discarded food lying around. Again, once the children are almost done with their crafts, it is completely permissible to start the cleanup. Don't forget to ask adults or older children for assistance. It really should take no time at all.

Food Allergies

These days a variety of food allergies are increasingly common. Reactions can be very severe, and in some cases even fatal. This is an important issue for you to discuss with parents and staff in relation to any activities that involve food. You'll find a reproducible form on the next page that you can use to make sure parents are aware of these issues. Give copies to parents or guardians prior to your story times, or at the beginning of the school year. Let them know that their children cannot participate in the story time snacks until you have received their signed forms. Keep them on file so they can be added to if necessary. This will help ensure that you are covered in case of an incident, and that you will be able to implement your programs without fear of an illness or adverse reaction.

Some of the most severe food allergies involve nuts. Some of the recipes included in this guide call for peanut butter. In a few cases, alternate craft or alternate ingredients have been provided. If you have several children with a specific allergy, you may wish to skip those programs altogether.

You may also ask parents what they use at home as substitutes for these items. For instance, is almond or apple butter acceptable in place of peanut butter? Since they live with these allergies, parents may have some great tips about alternatives.

Parents must also be cautioned that some of the candy items used in these recipes may have been processed in a plant that produces nut products. The form they fill out will let you know how severe their child's allergy is. Of course, most parents who have children with this type of severe allergy will let you know right away, as special precautions will have to be taken.

Make sure you have given everyone a form and have received them all back before proceeding with your programs. Again, keep them on file for future reference.

Wrap-up

The recipes in this guide were all personally tested by me on very willing story time participants during my career at the Chester Public Library. The programs are ready-made and can be implemented as is. They are easy for you or your staff to set up and execute; and I can vouch that the children will have a great time. However, they can also be tailored to whatever number of children you serve and adapted for fussy eaters or allergy sufferers. Also, new books get published every day, so you may want to add different titles to some of the programs.

The point of this guide is to facilitate putting on memorable programs for your children. The story times may be performed exactly the way they are for those with low budgets, little staff, and too many hats to wear, or, with some time and preplanning, you may easily add your own spin to them.

In short, have fun with them, as the children (and their parents) certainly will!

Food Allergy Form

In order for our organization to ensure your child's safe and active participation in our story time programs, we need to be aware of any food allergies he or she may have.

Please fill in the form below as completely as possible and return to _____ [name of organization] by _____ [date]. Failure to return the completed form may prevent your child from being able to participate in certain parts of our program, for his or her own safety. If you have more than one child who will be attending our programs, please fill out a separate form for EACH child. This form must be completed and SIGNED by the child's parent or legal guardian only.

If any changes to your child's health status occur, please notify us so that we may update this form.

Child's Name: _____

Address: _____

Date of Birth: _____

List of Foods the Child Is Allergic To (please list each one separately):

Food _____

Reaction type (rash, difficulty breathing, etc.): _____

Severe? ____ Yes ____ No

Substitution/Alternative (if applicable): _____

Food _____

Reaction type (rash, difficulty breathing, etc.): _____

Severe? ____ Yes ____ No

Substitution/Alternative (if applicable): _____

Food _____

Reaction type (rash, difficulty breathing, etc.): _____

Severe? ____ Yes ____ No

Substitution/Alternative (if applicable): _____

Food _____

Reaction type (rash, difficulty breathing, etc.): _____

Severe? ____ Yes ____ No

Substitution/Alternative (if applicable): _____

I understand that by signing this form I confirm that I have given complete and accurate information about my child's food allergies, and I am giving permission for my child to participate in the story time programs at _____ [name of organization].

Parent/Legal Guardian (print name): _____

Signature: _____

Date: _____

Staff Member Signature: _____

Date received: _____

From *Story Times Good Enough to Eat!: Thematic Programs with Edible Story Crafts*
by Melissa Rossetti Folini. Santa Barbara, CA: Libraries Unlimited. Copyright © 2010.

Chapter 1

Seasons: Fall

*T*his is a great theme to get children into the back to school frame of mind! Two of the titles suggested below are take-offs on the poem *'Twas the Night Before Christmas*, and children should have no trouble recognizing the familiar rhythms and rhymes. *The Wheels on the Bus* story, based on the popular song by the same name, encourages the children to participate by "singing" along with you. After enjoying these fun titles, children will get to make a school bus cupcake!

Suggested Titles

David Goes to School by David Shannon. Blue Sky Press, 1999. ISBN 0590480871.

The Night Before First Grade by Natasha Wing. Grosset & Dunlap, 2005. ISBN 0448437473.

The Night Before Kindergarten by Natasha Wing. Scholastic, 2001. ISBN 0448425009.

The Wheels on the Bus by Paul Zelinsky. Dutton, 1990. ISBN 0525446443.

School Bus Cupcake

Seasons: Fall

School Bus Cupcakes

Ingredients/Materials:

1 18½-ounce package cake mix (your choice of flavor). Follow package directions for making cupcakes.

1 15-ounce tub of white icing

1 9-ounce package waffle-printed vanilla wafers (1 full wafer for each child, precut into 2 pieces)

1 12-ounce package of chocolate chips, enough for 2 per child

2 or 3 .86-ounce tubes of black gel (optional)

Plastic knives

Cocktail napkins

Plastic cups

School Bus Cupcake Supplies

Instructions:

• Place 1 cupcake on a napkin in front of each child. Give them a knife, 2 precut wafer pieces (one wafer cut into ¾-inch by ¼-inch pieces) and 2 chocolate chips. Instruct them to cover the top of the cupcake (only) with the icing.

• Each child will then arrange the precut wafers on the top of the cupcake and place the 2 chocolate chips into the icing at the bottom of the wafers, points in, to represent wheels (as shown in the first photograph).

• The children may draw windows and lines on their buses using the black gel, if they wish.

From *Story Times Good Enough to Eat!: Thematic Programs with Edible Story Crafts* by Melissa Rossetti Folini. Santa Barbara, CA: Libraries Unlimited. Copyright © 2010.

NOTES

FIRE PREVENTION

*T*his is a very simple way to introduce children to the importance of fire safety. Fire Prevention Week is typically the second week in October. You may want to invite members of your local fire department to read to the children or bring in some of their gear to show what a firefighter looks like all dressed up. This helps to familiarize children with how a firefighter looks when combating a fire and allay their fears if they are involved in an emergency and actually see firefighters at work. It's fun for the children to try on the gear as well.

Suggested Titles

Arthur's Fire Drill by Marc Brown. Random House, 2000. ISBN 0679884769.

Dot the Fire Dog by Lisa Desimini. Blue Sky Press, 2001. ISBN 0439233224.

Firefighter Frank by Monica Wellington. Puffin, 2004. ISBN 0525470212.

Here Come Our Firefighters: Pop-up Book by Chris Demarest. Little, Simon, 2002. ISBN 068984834X.

Stop, Drop, and Roll by Margery Cuyler. Simon & Schuster, 2001. ISBN 0689843550.

Fire Prevention Snack

"Stop, Drop, and Roll" Treat Bags

Ingredients/Materials:

Snack-sized sandwich bags

1 bag or 7-ounce box of Gobstoppers™ candy

2 8-ounce bags, or 1 large plastic tub, of spice or gum drops (The bags are easier to find in your local grocery store candy section.)

1 15-ounce package of Tootsie Roll™ candies (both regular- and or mini-sized will work)

Lifesaver candies™ (either mini rolls, available around Halloween, or individually wrapped pieces) (optional)

Instructions:

- Give the children 1 bag each and instruct them to put 2–3 gum DROPs, GobSTOPers, and Tootsie ROLLs in their bags, then seal them up. They have just "stopped, dropped, and rolled."

- If you are using the Lifesavers, give the children a few to add to their bags. They will now have their own "police officers/firefighters" ("livesavers") to carry around.

- *Optional:* Before the story time, print fire safety tips on small cards or tags and punch a hole in each card and each sandwich bag. During the activity, have each child fasten a card to his or her bag using a twist tie. A sample tip is "If your clothes catch fire, **stop** where you are, **drop** to the ground, and **roll** to put the fire out."

NOTES

*H*alloween provides lots of options for crafts and stories. You may choose the traditional witches and scary story elements or focus on the more benign pumpkins and costumes. (Keep in mind that some populations have objections to witches and ghosts, and adapt your program accordingly.) The following list includes books for both options. Choose those that best suit your group.

Suggested Titles

Witches

These titles may also be used for a witch/wizard theme program. See the "witch/selection" hat craft under "Wizards" (in chapter 6).

Alice and Greta by Steven J. Simmons. Charlesbridge, 1999. ISBN 0881069744.

Alice and Greta's Color Magic by Steven J. Simmons. Dragonfly Books, 2003. ISBN 0375812458.

Miss Fiona's Stupendous Pumpkin Pies by Mark Kimball Moulton. Ideal's Children's Books, 2004. ISBN 0741208652.

The Night Before Halloween by Natasha Wing. Grosset & Dunlap, 1999. ISBN 0448419653.

Pumpkins

It's Pumpkin Time by Zoe Hall. Scholastic, 1999. ISBN 0590478338.

The Legend of Spookley the Square Pumpkin by Joe Troiano. Back Pack Press, 2001. ISBN 0760727546.

Pumpkin, Pumpkin by Jeanne Titherington. Greenwillow, 1990. ISBN 0688099300.

The Ugly Pumpkin by Dave Horowitz. Puffin, 2008. ISBN 0399242678.

Witch's Hand

Witch's Hands

Ingredients/Materials:

Disposable plastic (not latex) gloves, 1 per child (adult sizes work best for this craft)

1 16-ounce bag of popped popcorn (you may pop your own if preferred)

1 12-ounce bag of candy corn (5 pieces per child)

Twist ties, ribbon, or rubber bands

Plastic spider rings (optional)

Plastic or Styrofoam bowls (for serving popcorn "family style" in the middle of your craft table)

Witch's Hands Supplies

Instructions:

• Give each child 1 glove. Have the children place 1 piece of candy corn inside the tip of each finger to make the "nails."

• The children then fill the rest of the fingers and hand with the popcorn and tie the wrist closed with a twist tie, ribbon, or rubber band.

• If using the spider rings, have them place a ring on one of the fingers for an added creepy effect.

Pumpkin Cupcake

Pumpkin Cupcakes

Ingredients/Materials:

1 18½-ounce package cake mix (your choice of flavor). Follow package directions for making cupcakes.

1 15-ounce tub of white icing

Orange food coloring

1 16-ounce bag of pretzel sticks or nuggets (1 piece per child)

Black gel or chocolate chips (optional)

Plastic knives

Cocktail napkins

Plastic cups

Instructions:

- Ahead of time, tint the icing with 2–3 drops of the orange food coloring. The longer it sits the darker the color will be.

- Place one cupcake on a napkin in front of each child. Have the children frost the tops (only) of their cupcakes.

- Once this has been done, they should push their pretzel "stems" down into the center of the cupcake (as shown in the photo).

- *Optional:* Have the children make triangles or jack-o'-lantern faces with gel icing or use chocolate chips to create faces. If they do this, they should push the "stem" into the side of the cupcake, horizontally.

NOTES

THANKSGIVING

Most of us associate Thanksgiving with the start of the stressful holiday season and eating way too much turkey. This activity, with fun books and some rhyming text, helps introduce youngsters to the more common events that surround the day of the big bird—full bellies and football games!

Suggested Titles

I Know an Old Lady Who Swallowed a Pie by Alison Jackson. Puffin, 2002. ISBN 0140565957.

The Night Before Thanksgiving by Natasha Wing. Grosset & Dunlap, 2001. ISBN 0448425297.

Run Turkey Run by Diane Mayr. Walker Books for Young Adults, 2007. ISBN 0802796303.

Thanksgiving Wish by Michael J. Rosen. Blue Sky Press, 1999. ISBN 0590255630.

A Turkey for Thanksgiving by Eve Bunting. Clarion Books, 1995. ISBN 0899197930.

Turkey Cookie

Turkey Cookie

Ingredients/Materials:

1 13-ounce package of round fudge-striped shortbread cookies (1 per child)

1 15-ounce tub of chocolate icing

1 12-ounce bag of candy corn

1 13.8-ounce bag of chocolate kisses (unwrapped) (1 per child)

Plastic knives

Cocktail napkins/dessert plates

Plastic cups

Instructions:

- Give each child a cookie on a napkin or plate, plus a plastic knife. Have them turn the cookies over and frost the back with icing.

- Give each child a chocolate kiss to place in the center of the cookie, with the point facing up.

- Then give each child 4–5 candy corns to place around the edges of the cookie, point side out, for the turkey's "feathers."

- *Optional:* Use frosted cupcakes rather than cookies; just use more candy corn.

NOTES

Chapter 2

Seasons: Winter

CHINESE NEW YEAR

*T*his is a cultural program designed to give children a brief glimpse into another culture's traditions in a way they can understand and also have fun with. Chinese New Year follows the Chinese calendar and is therefore not on the same date every year. Check for the actual date, which traditionally falls in late January or early February.

This is a very simple program, in which the children will each be given a fortune cookie to take home. I usually have good luck getting the cookies donated by a local Chinese restaurant, but they are also sold in most grocery stores in the international foods section.

Suggested Titles

Dragon Dance: A Chinese New Year Lift-the-flap by Joan Holub. Puffin, 2003. ISBN 0142400009.

Lanterns and Firecrackers by Johnny Zucker. Barrons, 2004. ISBN 0764126687.

Sam and the Lucky Money by Karen Chinn. Lee & Low Books, 1995. ISBN 1880000539.

This Next New Year by Janet S. Wong. Farrar, Strauss, & Giroux, 2000. ISBN 0374355037.

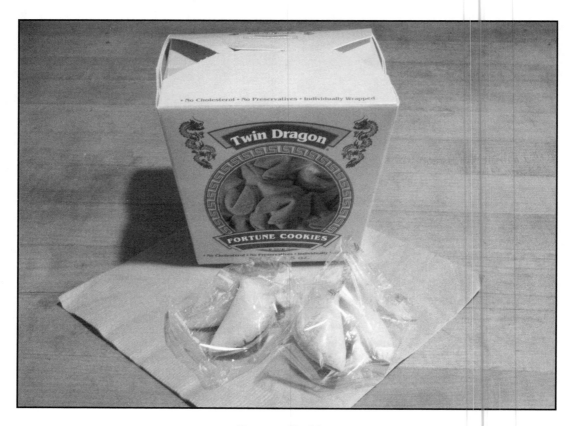

Fortune Cookies

Fortune Cookies

Ingredients/Materials:

Individually wrapped fortune cookies, 1 for each child

Instructions:

- After reading the stories, give each child a fortune cookie. If the fortunes have Chinese words or phrases on the back, have the children practice speaking them with the pronunciation guides provided.

- *Optional:* Make a "dragon face" mask out of a paper plate, then have the children stand in a line behind you (or another "leader" who is wearing the mask). Unfurl red crepe paper streamers on each side of the line and have the children hold on to them and wave their arms up and down as they follow the leader in a "dragon dance." If you think the streamers will rip too easily, have the children stay still and give them each two lengths of streamer to tie around their wrists instead.

Materials for optional activity:

1 paper plate "mask" with eye holes, colored red and black

Crayons/markers

1–2 rolls of red crepe paper streamers

From *Story Times Good Enough to Eat!: Thematic Programs with Edible Story Crafts* by Melissa Rossetti Folini. Santa Barbara, CA: Libraries Unlimited. Copyright © 2010.

NOTES

CHRISTMAS

*C*hristmas is probably the most well-known and widely celebrated of all the holidays in the Western hemisphere. There are a myriad of books to choose from for this activity, depending on which aspects of the holiday you are able to share in your setting. (Keep in mind that some populations object to celebrating this religious holiday, and adapt your program accordingly.) The books listed here are those I found to be especially fun. Some are traditional, covering some of the better known stories that children have heard. These books are easy to read aloud to keep the children's interest. Feel free to adjust the titles for your particular group of children.

Suggested Titles

Christmas Lights by Ann Fearrington. Houghton Mifflin, 1996. ISBN 0395710367.

Hark! The Aardvark Angels Sing: A Story of Christmas Mail by Teri Sloat. Putnam, 2001. ISBN 0399233717.

How the Reindeer Got Their Antlers by Geraldine McCaughrean. Holiday House, 2000. ISBN 0823415627.

Olive, the Other Reindeer by J. Otto Seibold and Vivian Walsh. Chronicle Books, 1997. ISBN 0811818071.

Santa's New Suit by Laura Radar. HarperCollins, 2000. ISBN 0060284390.

'Twas the Night Before Christmas by Clement C. Moore. Grosset & Dunlap, 1981. ISBN 0448029359. There are several beautifully illustrated versions of this classic story. Choose one that works in your situation.

Wombat Divine by Mem Fox. Harcourt, Brace & Jovanovich, 1996. ISBN 0152014160.

Reindeer Cookie

Reindeer Cookies

Ingredients/Materials:

Round chocolate cream-filled cookies, enough for 1 per child

1 15-ounce tub of chocolate icing

1 12-ounce bag of chocolate chips OR

1 15-ounce box of raisins

Mini pretzel twists or sticks, enough for 2–4 per child

1 container of small round cinnamon dot candy (optional)

Plastic knives

Cocktail napkins/dessert plates

Plastic cups

Instructions:

- Give each child 1 cookie on a napkin or plate and a plastic knife.

- Have the children frost the top and sides of the cookie with the icing.

- Give the children 2 pretzels twists (or 4 pretzel sticks) each and have them add a bit of extra icing to the pretzels, then push the pretzels into one edge of the cookie for "antlers."

- Give the children 2 chocolate chips each to place point side down into the frosting on the front of the cookie for "eyes." They may also use raisins.

- If they want to make the famous red-nosed reindeer, give them each 1 red cinnamon candy to use as the "nose."

From *Story Times Good Enough to Eat!: Thematic Programs with Edible Story Crafts*
by Melissa Rossetti Folini. Santa Barbara, CA: Libraries Unlimited. Copyright © 2010.

Candy Cane Reindeer

Seasons: Winter

Candy Cane Reindeer

Optional craft for very young children, or when you are pressed for time.

Ingredients/Materials:

Large candy canes (individually wrapped), 1 per child

10- to 12-inch pipe cleaners, preferably brown (1 per child), cut in half

Small red pom-poms (optional)

Wiggly eyes (optional)

Instructions:

- Give each child 1 candy cane and 1 pipe cleaner.

- Instruct the children to wrap each half of the pipe cleaner around the upper curved part of the candy cane, being careful not to twist to hard. Have them twist 2 times and bend the stems to form "antlers."

- If using the small red pom-poms for the nose or the wiggly eyes, you will need glue (the white, nontoxic kind), patience, and more time.

- *Note:* Caution the children that only the candy cane, once it is unwrapped, is edible. Instruct them not to eat the pipe cleaner, nose, or eyes.

NOTES

MARDI GRAS

*A*lthough technically a religious holiday (Shrove Tuesday), Mardi Gras has become a multiday festival better known for its colorful costume parade, with its beads, coins, and masks. Through a few quirky books with vibrant illustrations, children can learn about the famous "Fat Tuesday" that is part of the celebration.

This event does not fall on the same dates every year, so check for the actual dates that it will take place on from year to year.

Suggested Titles

Gaston Goes to Mardi Gras by James Rice. Pelican Publishing, 1987. ISBN 0882891588.

Jenny Giraffe's Mardi Gras Ride by Cecilia Casrill Dartez. Pelican Publishing, 1997. ISBN 1565541820.

Mimi and Jean-Paul's Cajun Mardi Gras by Alice Couvillon and Elizabeth Moore. Pelican Publishing, 1996. ISBN 1565540697.

Mimi's First Mardi Gras by Alice Couvillon and Elizabeth Moore. Pelican Publishing, 1999. ISBN 088289840X.

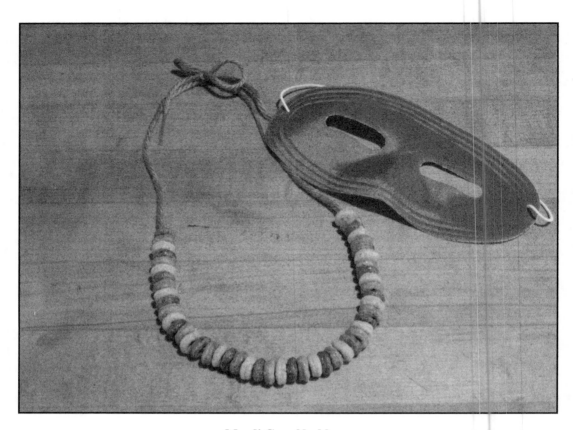

Mardi Gras Necklace

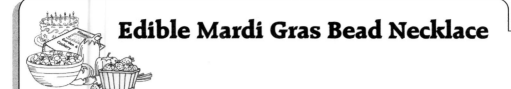

Edible Mardi Gras Bead Necklace

Ingredients/Materials:

> 1 14-ounce box of multicolored cereal rings
>
> String, ribbon, or cord (cut into 25- to 30-inch lengths), 1 piece per child
>
> Styrofoam or plastic bowls, 1 for every 4–5 children

Instructions:

- Fill several Styrofoam bowls with the dry cereal. Place them in the middle of your craft area.

- Give each child a piece of string. Instruct the children to slide 20 or so pieces of cereal onto the string to form a necklace. Help them tie a knot in the end. They can then wear the necklace, and eat it.

- *Optional:* If you can find colorful masks, usually available at your local party store, give 1 to each of the children to wear after they have made their necklaces. If time allows, have the children decorate their masks, using glue, assorted sequins, stones, or feathers. (Of course the masks would be for decoration only, in no way edible.)

- *Note:* Caution the children to eat just the cereal, not the string.

From *Story Times Good Enough to Eat!: Thematic Programs with Edible Story Crafts*
by Melissa Rossetti Folini. Santa Barbara, CA: Libraries Unlimited. Copyright © 2010.

NOTES

PRESIDENT'S DAY

*T*his is a very simple program that teaches children the reason for the traditional Monday holiday in February, when we celebrate the birthdays of Presidents Abraham Lincoln and George Washington. In this program, the stories are more biographical than picture books, and the snack is an individual cherry pie in honor of the legend of George Washington being truthful about chopping down a cherry tree.

For a theme-related, quick, nonfood craft, you might give the children a penny, a piece of white copy paper, and a pencil and have them do a coin rubbing of Abraham Lincoln's head. When I do this activity, I give children the pennies to take home. You can also do this with a quarter, but of course that's more expensive to give away!

Suggested Titles

Abe Lincoln: The Boy Who Loved Books by Kay Winters and Nancy Carpenter. Simon & Schuster, 2002. ISBN 1416912681.

George Washington's Teeth by Deborah Chandra. Square Fish Books, 2007. ISBN 0312376049.

It's President's Day by Anne Rockwell. HarperCollins, 2007. ISBN 0060501944.

Meet George Washington by Patricia A. Pingry. Candy Cane Press, 2000. ISBN 0824941314.

Mr. Lincoln's Whiskers by Karen Winnick. Boyds Mill Press, 1996. ISBN 1563978059.

Stand Tall, Abe Lincoln by Judith St. George. Philomel, 2008. ISBN 0399241744.

Cherry Pie

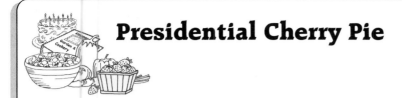

Presidential Cherry Pie

Ingredients/Materials:

Twin-wrapped cherry pie snacks, enough for 1 pie per child

Cocktail napkins

Paper American flag toothpicks (optional)

Instructions:

- Open the packages and give each child 1 pie on a napkin.

- *Optional:* Give each child an American flag tooth pick to place in the middle of each pie, making it a patriotic cherry pie.

- *Optional:* Give each child 3–4 mini Tootsie Roll™ candies. As you pass them out, explain that these are "Lincoln Logs." This way, you can have snacks to represent both presidents!

From *Story Times Good Enough to Eat!: Thematic Programs with Edible Story Crafts* by Melissa Rossetti Folini. Santa Barbara, CA: Libraries Unlimited. Copyright © 2010.

NOTES

ST. PATRICK'S DAY

*N*early everyone pretends to be Irish on this famous day in March. This program explores the myths and legends of St. Patrick's Day with entertaining picture books, and little leprechaun treats to take home.

Suggested Titles

A Fine St. Patrick's Day by Susan Wojciechowski. Random House, 2004. ISBN 0375923861.

A Leprechaun's St. Patrick's Day by Sarah Kirwan Blazek. Pelican Publishing, 1997. ISBN 1565542371.

Lucky O'Leprechaun by Jana Dillon. Pelican Publishing, 2000. ISBN 1565543335.

St. Patrick's Day in the Morning by Eve Bunting. Clarion Books, 1980. ISBN 0395290988.

Leprechaun Treats

Leprechaun Treats

Ingredients/Materials:

> 1 13.9 -ounce box of "Magic Stars" cereal
>
> Snack-sized zipper seal bags, 1 per child
>
> Green Tic-tacs™ (optional)
>
> Styrofoam or plastic bowls

Instructions:

- Divide the cereal among the Styrofoam bowls and place the bowls in the middle of your craft table.

- Give each child a snack bag, making sure it is open.

- Have the children fill the bags almost to the top with handfuls of the cereal.

- Have the children seal their bags and take them home. Tell them that if they leave the bags out, maybe they will be visited by a wee leprechaun.

- *Optional:* For older children, have them add 1 or 2 green Tic-tacs™ to their bags.

NOTES

VALENTINE'S DAY

*T*his fun day in February is filled with hearts and flowers—and of course chocolate! These books explore all the well-known aspects of the holiday, from flowers to cards.

Suggested Titles

The Ballad of Valentine by Alison Jackson. Dutton, 2002. ISBN 0525467203.

The Best Thing About Valentines by Eleanor Hudson. Cartwheel, 2004. ISBN 0439521092.

Biscuit's Valentine's Day by Alyssa Satin Capucilli. HarperFestival, 2001. ISBN 069401222X.

The Night Before Valentine's Day by Natasha Wing. Grosset & Dunlap, 2000. ISBN 0448421887.

Valentine's Day by Anne Rockwell. HarperCollins, 2001. ISBN 006028515x.

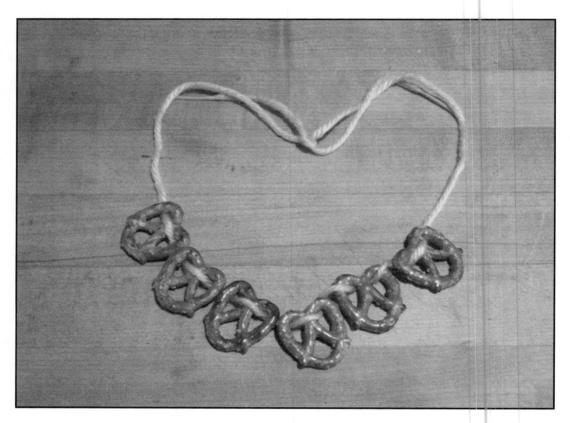

Hearts Necklace

Edible Hearts Necklace

Ingredients/Materials:

Mini pretzel twists, enough for 6–8 per child

Ribbon, string, or cord (cut into 20- to 25-inch lengths), preferably red or pink, 1 per child

Instructions:

- Give each child a piece of ribbon or string.

- Give the children each 6–8 pretzel twists and have them "thread" the string through the top 2 holes of the pretzel twists.

- Have the children center the string and then tie a knot in the end. They now have a string of "hearts" necklace to eat or share.

- *Note:* Be sure to caution the children that the string is not edible.

From *Story Times Good Enough to Eat!: Thematic Programs with Edible Story Crafts*
by Melissa Rossetti Folini. Santa Barbara, CA: Libraries Unlimited. Copyright © 2010.

NOTES

WINTER/SNOW

*N*o one likes to be stuck inside, but if you live where there is snow, there are bound to be bad weather days. These books show the fun side of that fluffy stuff, and the children may make one of two crafts celebrating favorite winter pastimes.

Suggested Titles

It's Winter by Linda Glaser. Millbrook Press, 2002. ISBN 0761316809.

Snow by Cynthia Rylant. Harcourt Children's Books, 2008. ISBN 9780152053031.

Snow Day! by Lester L. Laminack. Peachtree Publishing, 2007. ISBN 1561454184.

The Snow Parade by Barbara Brenner. Crown Publishing, 1984. ISBN 0517552108.

Stella, Queen of the Snow by Mary-Louise Gay. Groundwood, 2000. ISBN 0888994044.

Edible Snowman

Edible Snowman

Ingredients/Materials:

Powdered sugar donut holes, enough for 2 per child

Mini powdered sugar donuts, enough for 1 per child

1 16-ounce bag of pretzel sticks (or can of potato sticks)

2–3 0.68-ounce tubes of black gel (optional)

Cocktail napkins

Instructions:

- Give each child a napkin, 2 donut holes, and 1 mini donut.

- Give the children each 1 pretzel stick and tell them to stick each end of the stick into the donut holes to hold them together. They can then set the donut holes on top of the mini donut.

- Have the children make a nose and arms by breaking up pretzel sticks and pushing the pieces into the top donut hole.

- *Optional:* Have the children make faces and buttons with the black gel (keep in mind that the gel does not always stick well to the powdered sugar).

From *Story Times Good Enough to Eat!: Thematic Programs with Edible Story Crafts* by Melissa Rossetti Folini. Santa Barbara, CA: Libraries Unlimited. Copyright © 2010.

Edible Snowshoes

Edible Snowshoes

This optional craft contains peanut butter, so it will not be suitable for those with nut allergies.

Ingredients/Materials:

Peanut-shaped peanut butter cookies, enough for 2 per child

Pretzel sticks, enough for 2 per child

Mini marshmallows, enough for 2 per child

2–3 0.68-ounce tubes of black gel icing

Cocktail napkins

Instructions:

- Give each child 2 cookies on a napkin, 2 pretzel sticks, and 2 mini marshmallows.

- Have them push 1 marshmallow onto the end of each pretzel stick. These are the "poles."

- Have them use the gel to make lines in a criss-cross pattern on the top of each cookie.

- They have just created their very own pair of "snowshoes!"

From *Story Times Good Enough to Eat!: Thematic Programs with Edible Story Crafts* by Melissa Rossetti Folini. Santa Barbara, CA: Libraries Unlimited. Copyright © 2010.

NOTES

Chapter 3

Seasons: Spring

CINCO DE MAYO

*I*ntroduce children to a cultural holiday by celebrating Mexican Independence Day with them on May 5. They will have fun making a typical Mexican souvenir, a sombrero (edible, of course!)

Suggested Titles

Celebrate! It's Cinco de Mayo by Janice Levy. Albert Whitman, 2007. ISBN 0807511773 Bilingual Edition.

Celebrate Cinco de Mayo with the Mexican Hat Dance by Alma F. Ada and F. Isabel Campoy. Alfaguara Infantil, 2006. ISBN 1598201301.

Max Celebrates Cinco de Mayo by Adria F. Worsham. Picture Window Books, 2008. ISBN 1404847596.

Sugar Cookie Sombrero

Sugar Cookie Sombreros

Ingredients/Materials:

1 16-ounce roll of sugar cookie dough (or prepare dough from a dry mix)

Gum or spice drops, Dots™, or juju fruits, enough for 1 per child (NOTE: Select candy stores sell colored gummy mini Mexican hats. If you can find those, they would be great to use in the middle of the hats, but the other options are less expensive and much easier to obtain.)

1 15-ounce tub of white icing

Plastic knives

Cocktail napkins

Plastic cups

Food coloring (optional)

Multicolored nonpareils/sprinkles (optional)

Instructions:

- Bake the sugar cookies prior to your story time. For more festive cookies, tint the dough with food coloring.

- Give each child 1 cookie on a napkin and a plastic knife. Have the children place a dot of frosting in the center of the cookie.

- Give each child 1 gum drop or other candy to place on the frosting (as shown in the picture).

- To create "fringe" on the hats, have the children frost the outer edges of their cookies and roll them in nonpareils or jimmies.

From *Story Times Good Enough to Eat!: Thematic Programs with Edible Story Crafts* by Melissa Rossetti Folini. Santa Barbara, CA: Libraries Unlimited. Copyright © 2010.

NOTES

*T*his program focuses on the nontraditional, nonreligious, child-friendly aspect of the Easter holiday with the Easter Bunny and egg hunt theme. The program can easily be combined with an egg hunt. To save money, buy plastic eggs after Easter on sale, then save them for the next year. To make sure the eggs are returned after the children find them, I put in them not only candy, but also a ticket for a special prize in one egg. This ensures the eggs will all be opened and returned, so you can collect them and use them again next year.

Keep in mind that some populations are averse to celebrating religious holidays, so be aware of your community and adapt the program accordingly. For example, you may want to call it a "springtime celebration" rather than an Easter celebration.

Suggested Titles

The Country Bunny and the Little Gold Shoes by Du Bose Heyward. Sandpiper, 1974. ISBN 0395185572.

Cranberry Easter by Wende Devlin and Harry Devlin. Four Winds Press, 1990. ISBN 002729935X

The Easter Bunny That Overslept by Priscilla Otto Friedrich. HarperCollins, 2002. ISBN 0060296543.

Easter Mice by Bethany Roberts. Clarion Books, 2003. ISBN 0618164553.

The Night Before Easter by Natasha Wing. Grosset & Dunlap, 1999. ISBN 0448418738.

Carrot Bag

Carrot Bag

Ingredients/Materials:

Gallon-sized food storage bags (or carrot-shaped bags; see below), 1 per child

Green ribbon cut into 6-inch pieces, or green twist ties, 1 per bag

1 15-ounce bag of cheese curls, puffs, or balls or orange jelly beans, orange-coated chocolate candy pieces, or orange-coated peanut butter candies

Large plastic or Styrofoam bowls

Instructions:

- Divide the cheese curls or puffs among a few large bowls and place the bowls in the middle of your craft table. Two large bowls should supply 10–12 children.

- Give each child a plastic bag and a tie.

- Have the children fill their bags on an angle to form a carrot shape, starting by putting 1 cheese curl in the point or corner of the bag. They should then fill the bags about three-quarters full, so there is enough empty bag left to be tied off to form the leaves.

- The children then tie off the bags to form the leaves, using the twist ties.

- Many candy supply stores (and even Wal-Mart) carry carrot-shaped bags in packages, complete with green ribbon and cut-out leaves.

- *Note:* The cheese curls are the largest option and fill the bags most quickly, but you may prefer to use the candy. If you use the peanut butter candy, prior to story time, make sure no one in the group has nut allergies.

From *Story Times Good Enough to Eat!: Thematic Programs with Edible Story Crafts*
by Melissa Rossetti Folini. Santa Barbara, CA: Libraries Unlimited. Copyright © 2010.

NOTES

MAPLE SUGAR/SYRUP

*W*hen the sap buckets start popping up on local trees, the snow begins to melt, or the rain stops falling, it's a great time to put on this program. It's very fast and simple and gives the children a glimpse into the mysterious silver buckets.

Suggested Titles

Maple Syrup Season by Ann Purmell. Holiday House, 2008. ISBN 082341891X.

Sugar Snow by Laura Ingalls Wilder and Doris Ettlinger. HarperCollins, 1998. ISBN 0060259329.

Sugarbush Spring by Marsha Wilson Chall. Lothrop & Lee, 2000. ISBN 0668149081.

Sugaring by Jessie Haas. Greenwillow, 1996. ISBN 0688142001.

Maple Leaf Cookies

Maple Leaf Cookies

Ingredients/Materials:

Maple leaf–shaped cream cookies, enough for 1 or 2 per child

Cocktail napkins

Apple juice or cider and small paper cups for serving (optional)

Instructions:

- For this very simple snack, give each child a napkin and 1 or 2 cookies. These cookies are shaped like maple leaves and have a maple cream filling. They can be found in some major chain grocery stores or can be obtained through the Dollar Tree store chain.

- If you happen to live in New England and have a sugar house nearby, you can arrange for staff members to come speak to your group. They might even donate some of their leaf-shaped maple candies, but keep in mind that these candies are typically small, so watch the younger children for choking.

- If you have chosen to use apple juice, give each child a small cup of juice. These can be their "sap buckets."

- If you are unable to obtain the maple leaf cookies, here are a couple of other options:

- Bake sugar cookies in the shape of maple leaves and have the children frost them and cover them with sprinkles. You will need the cookies, vanilla icing, plastic knives, napkins, and sprinkles.

- Give the children small cups ("buckets") of vanilla ice cream, then have them pour maple syrup over the ice cream and watch the "sap run." For this you will need small cups, 1–2 cartons of vanilla ice cream, plastic spoons, and a bottle of maple syrup.

From *Story Times Good Enough to Eat!: Thematic Programs with Edible Story Crafts* by Melissa Rossetti Folini. Santa Barbara, CA: Libraries Unlimited. Copyright © 2010.

NOTES

MUD

*M*ost parts of the country that experience a snowy winter also have a muddy season come spring. This program celebrates the mess that kids love to make and allows them to make some mud that is actually edible!

Suggested Titles

I Love Mud and Mud Loves Me by Vicki Stephens. Scholastic, 1994. ISBN 0590273817.

Mud by Mary Lyn Ray. Voyager Books, 1996. ISBN 015256263X.

Mud Puddle by Robert Munsch. Annick Press, 1982. ISBN 1550374680.

Finished Mud Cups

Mud Cups

Ingredients/Materials:

    1 2.1-ounce box of chocolate instant pudding mix

    Crushed chocolate cookie crumbs

    Gummy worms

    8- to 9-ounce plastic cups, 1 for each child

    Plastic spoons

    Styrofoam or plastic bowls

Mud Cup Supplies

Instructions:

- Prepare the pudding ahead of time (a day or a few hours ahead) and refrigerate it. You may leave it in one big container and let the children spoon their portions into their plastic cups, or fill the cups three-quarters full ahead of time.

- Divide the other ingredients among the Styrofoam bowls and place the bowls in the middle of your craft table, 1 bowl of each ingredient for every 4–5 children. Give each child 1 cup of pudding and a spoon.

- If the children are filling their own cups, have them fill them three-quarters full. They will then spoon the crushed cookies (dirt) on top and drape 1 or 2 gummy worms over the side of the cup. Then let them dig in!

From *Story Times Good Enough to Eat!: Thematic Programs with Edible Story Crafts* by Melissa Rossetti Folini. Santa Barbara, CA: Libraries Unlimited. Copyright © 2010.

NOTES

Chapter 4

Seasons: Summer

CAMPING

*H*ere's a fun way to bring the joy of sleeping outdoors inside, without all the ants or the mosquitoes! You may even want to pitch a small tent in your reading area, if you have space. At the end of the stories each child gets to make their very own edible campfire.

Suggested Titles

Arthur Goes to Camp by Marc Brown. Little, Brown, 1982. ISBN 0316112186.

A Camping Spree with Mr. Magee by Chris Van Dusen. Chronicle Books, 2003. ISBN 0811836037.

Stella & Roy Go Camping by Ashley Wolff. Dutton, 1999. ISBN 0525458646.

Tacky Goes to Camp by Helen Lester. Houghton Mifflin, 2001. ISBN 97806189881329.

Edible Campfire

Edible Campfire

Ingredients/Materials:

    Round fudge-striped shortbread cookies, enough for 1 per child

    1 15-ounce tub of chocolate icing

    Candy corn, enough for 4–5 pieces per child

    Pretzel sticks, enough for 3–4 per child

    Mini marshmallows, enough for 1 per child (optional)

    Plastic knives

    Cocktail napkins

    Plastic cups

Instructions:

- Give each child one cookie on a napkin and a plastic knife.
- Have the children place a small amount of icing around the hole in the center of their cookies. They should NOT frost the entire cookie.
- Give the children 4–5 pieces of candy corn each and have them arrange them point side up in the frosting, in a circle around the center of their cookies. This is the "fire."
- Give them 3–4 pretzel sticks each to lay across the cookies in between the candy corn pieces. This is the "kindling."
- *Optional:* Give each child an additional pretzel stick and a mini marshmallow. Tell them to push the marshmallow gently onto the end of the pretzel. They can now "roast" marshmallows over their campfires!

From *Story Times Good Enough to Eat!: Thematic Programs with Edible Story Crafts*
by Melissa Rossetti Folini. Santa Barbara, CA: Libraries Unlimited. Copyright © 2010.

NOTES

SUNFLOWERS

*T*his is a fun way to capture the magic of that perennial summer staple, the sunflower. After a couple of stories about these mammoth blooms, children will enjoy making a sunflower they can eat!

Suggested Titles

Max Loves Sunflowers by Ken Wilson-Max. David Bennett Books, 1998. ISBN 0786804130.

A Sunflower as Big as the Sun by Shan Ellentuck. Doubleday, 1968. LCCN 68-11200.

Sunflower House by Eve Bunting. Harcourt Children's Books, 1980. ISBN 0152004831.

This Is the Sunflower by Lola M. Schaefer. Greenwillow, 2000. ISBN 0688164137.

Sunflower Cupcake

Sunflower Cupcakes

Ingredients/Materials:

1 18½-ounce package cake mix (your choice of flavor). Follow package directions for making cupcakes.

1 15-ounce tub of white icing and 3–4 drops of yellow food coloring, OR lemon-flavored icing

Chocolate chips, enough for 10–12 per child

Candy corn, enough for 12 per child

Plastic knives

Cocktail napkins/dessert plates

Plastic cups

Instructions:

• Before the story time, tint the white icing with the food coloring. The longer it sits, the darker it will be.

• Give each child 1 cupcake on a napkin/plate and a plastic knife. Have them frost the top (only) of the cupcakes.

• Then have them arrange the chocolate chips in the center of their cupcakes with the points facing upward.

• After that, have them take 12 candy corn pieces and place them flat, point side facing away from the chips, around the edges of their cupcakes.

• *Optional:* Use round sugar cookies instead of cupcakes; decorating instructions remain the same.

• *Optional:* To make a sunflower cake instead of individual cupcakes, use an 8-inch round yellow cake with yellow icing. Put chocolate chips in the middle but instead of candy corn, use yellow marshmallow chicks around the edge. This is a cute idea for a sunflower theme as well as an Easter dessert.

From *Story Times Good Enough to Eat!: Thematic Programs with Edible Story Crafts*
by Melissa Rossetti Folini. Santa Barbara, CA: Libraries Unlimited. Copyright © 2010.

NOTES

Chapter 5

Insects and Other Animals

*T*his simple program features a great rhyming book that encourages children to participate. They then make the old standby snack/craft "Ants on a Log." There are many variations you can use for this snack to make it more kid friendly. Several options, which take into account children's food preferences and allergies, follow.

Suggested Titles

Hey Little Ant by Phillip M. Hoose and Hannah Hoose. Tricycle Press, 2004. ISBN 1883672546.

I Saw an Ant on the Railroad Track by Joshua Prince. Sterling Publishing, 2006. ISBN 1402721838.

The Little Ant by Daniel Novak. Riverbank Press, 1994. ISBN 0874066891.

Two Bad Ants by Chris Van Allsburg. Houghton Mifflin Books for Children, 1998. ISBN 0395486688.

Ants on a Log

Insects and Other Animals

Ants on a Log

Ingredients/Materials:

    3-inch celery sticks, 1 per child

    1 8-ounce tub of spreadable cream cheese

    Raisins, enough for 3–4 per child

    Plastic knives

    Cocktail napkins

    Plastic cups

Instructions:

- Give each child 1 celery stick on a napkin and a plastic knife. (Purchase these already cleaned, cut, and sliced in the vegetable section of your grocery store, or buy whole stalks, trim off the leaves, and cut them up.)

- Have the children spread the cream cheese down the center of their sticks and place 3–4 raisins in a row on top of the cream cheese.

Variations:

- Instead of celery, use carrot sticks (small), pretzel rods (cut in half), or rolled wafer cookies.

- Instead of cream cheese, use peanut butter (check for nut allergies), spreadable cheddar cheese, ranch or vegetable flavor dips, or plain sour cream (caution: these will be a bit runnier).

- Instead of raisins, use chocolate chips, carob chips, or chocolate sprinkles.

NOTES

BEARS (TEDDY)

*C*hildren love teddy bears, and this is a fun program that can also be done as a nighttime story time, where the children are encouraged to come in their pajamas and bring their favorite Teddy bears with them. These books include some tales and legends of both real and beloved teddy bears. *The Teddy Bears Picnic* may also be used as a song to get the children involved. Some bookstores and libraries carry the CD version of the story, with the accompanying music.

Suggested Titles

Corduroy by Don Freeman. Puffin, 1976. ISBN 0140501738.

The Legend of Sleeping Bear by Kathy-Jo Wargin. Sleeping Bear Press, 1998. ISBN 188694735X.

The Teddy Bear by David McPhail. Henry Holt, 2005. ISBN 0805078827.

The Teddy Bear's Picnic by Jimmy Kennedy. Henry Holt, 1997. ISBN 0805053492.

Sleeping Teddy Bears

Insects and Other Animals

Sleeping Teddy Bears

Ingredients/Materials:

Snack-sized zipper close bags, 1 per child

Bear-shaped graham crackers, enough for several per child

Mini marshmallows, enough for several per child (optional)

Styrofoam bowls or large plastic mixing bowls

Instructions:

• Put the marshmallows and the crackers into bowls, 1 bowl per ingredient for every 4–5 children, and place the bowls in the middle of your craft table.

• Give each child a snack bag.

• Have the children put 1 or 2 handfuls of the crackers (and mini marshmallows, if you're using them) in their bags. They now have a bedtime bear snack to take home.

From *Story Times Good Enough to Eat!: Thematic Programs with Edible Story Crafts* by Melissa Rossetti Folini. Santa Barbara, CA: Libraries Unlimited. Copyright © 2010.

NOTES

DINOSAURS

*D*inosaurs have been favorites of children since the Ice Age (almost)! These titles follow dinosaurs in prehistoric times and in the modern age as well, along with some dinosaur facts thrown in. After hearing a few stories about these perennial prehistoric favorites, children will go on a dino dig for fossils of their very own!

Suggested Titles

Big Old Bones: A Dinosaur's Tale by Carol Carrick and Donald Carrick. Sandpiper, 1992. ISBN 0395615828.

Dinosaur Parade: A Spectacle of Prehistoric Proportions by Kelly Milner Halls. Lark Books/Sterling, 2008. ISBN 1600592678.

A Night in the Dinosaur Graveyard: A Prehistoric Story by Wayne Anderson and A. J. Wood. Templar, 1995. ISBN 1898784035.

When Dinosaurs Go to School by Linda Martin. Chronicle Books, 2002. ISBN 0811835146.

Dino Dig

Insects and Other Animals

Dino Dig

Ingredients/Materials:

1 2.1-ounce box of instant chocolate pudding mix
White chocolate chips, enough for 6–8 per child
Crushed chocolate cookie crumbs
Plastic cups
Plastic spoons
Styrofoam or plastic bowls

Dino Dig Supplies

Instructions:

- Prepare the pudding ahead of time (a day or a few hours ahead) and refrigerate it. You may leave it in one big container and let the children spoon their portions into their plastic cups, or fill the cups ahead of time.

- Give each child 1 cup and a plastic spoon.

- Divide the cookie crumbs and white chocolate chips among the bowls, 1 bowl of each ingredient for every 4–5 children, and place the bowls in the middle of your craft table.

- Have the children stir 6–8 white chocolate chips (bones) into their pudding, then cover the top with the crushed cookie crumbs (dirt.)

- They can now go dig up some fossils!

From *Story Times Good Enough to Eat!: Thematic Programs with Edible Story Crafts* by Melissa Rossetti Folini. Santa Barbara, CA: Libraries Unlimited. Copyright © 2010.

NOTES

DOGS

*D*ogs are extremely popular, and many households have one. There are many great dog stories to choose from for a program on this theme. The Clifford, Sally, and Mrs. Larue series all have many titles to choose from. You could do a program all about Clifford or you mix and match the stories. This program has a mixture of both new and well-loved dog characters, and will let the kids eat some human "dog food" when they're done.

Suggested Titles

Bad Dog, Marley! by John Grogan. HarperCollins, 2007. ISBN 9780061171154.

Clifford and His Friends by Norman Bridwell. Cartwheel Books, 2007. ISBN 0545000645.

Dear Mrs. LaRue: Letters from Obedience School by Mark Teague. Scholastic, 2002. ISBN 0439206634.

Dog Breath by Dav Pilkey. Scholastic/Blue Sky, 1994. ISBN 0590474669.

Sally Goes to the Beach by Stephen Huneck. Harry N. Abrams, 2001. ISBN 0810941864.

"Puppy Chow"

Insects and Other Animals

"Puppy Chow"

Note: Be sure to double check for any nut allergies before doing this activity.

Ingredients/Materials:

1 14-ounce box of Chex™-type cereal

1 28-ounce jar of creamy peanut butter (at room temperature)

1 16-ounce box of confectioner's sugar

Plastic spoons

Plastic cups

Cocktail napkins

Instructions:

- This is a VERY MESSY craft. You can make it ahead of time and simply let the children scoop some into plastic cups or even small Styrofoam cereal bowls, which gives the children the illusion of eating out of a dog bowl.

- If you want the children to make their own, give them each a plastic cup and a plastic spoon.

- Have the children scoop enough cereal into their cups to fill them three-quarters full, leaving room for mixing.

- Next have the children add a spoonful or two of confectioner's sugar and 2–3 spoonfuls of peanut butter. Then they can mix it all together and enjoy!

- To mix the peanut butter takes some time, a little help from an adult, and a LOT of napkins!

- *Note:* Please remind children that although this is a "puppy chow" they CAN eat, they should NOT eat any regular pet food they might find at home.

NOTES

LADYBUGS

*L*adybugs are very cute and unobtrusive insects, which some believe are good luck should they land on you. Following some creative stories celebrating New Hampshire's state insect, the children will create their very own ladybugs.

Suggested Titles

The Grouchy Ladybug by Eric Carle. HarperCollins, 1996. ISBN 0064434508.

Lady Adrian by Amy Bryson. PCP Publishing, 2002. ISBN 0971109303.

Ladybugs Birthday by Steve Metzger. Scholastic, 1998. ISBN 0590025996.

Two Little Ladybugs by Larry Purcell. Tate Publishing, 2008. ISBN 1606041665

Edible Ladybug

Insects and Other Animals

Edible Ladybugs

Ingredients/Materials:

Round cream-filled chocolate cookies, enough for 1 per child

1 15-ounce tub of white icing and 5–6 drops of food coloring

Chocolate chips, enough for 5–6 per child

Licorice "whips" cut into 1-inch strips, enough for 2–3 per cookie

1 0.68-ounce tube of black gel (optional)

Plastic knives

Cocktail napkins/dessert plates

Plastic cups

Instructions:

- Prior to story time (a few hours or a day ahead), tint the icing with the food coloring. You want it to be dark red, and the longer the icing sits, the darker it will be.

- Give each child 1 cookie on a napkin/plate and a plastic knife.

- Have the children cover the top and sides of their cookies with the red frosting.

- Give the children 5–6 chocolate chips each to place on top of the cookie. They may use two for eyes if they wish.

- Give them each 2 licorice pieces to use for antennas. They should push them into one side of the cookie through the frosting and into the cream center.

- *Optional:* Have the children place a third strip of licorice down the middle of the cookie on the top to show the separation between the two "wings" (as in the picture).

- *Optional:* In place of the string licorice or chocolate chips, use the black gel to make the dots and the line down the center.

From *Story Times Good Enough to Eat!: Thematic Programs with Edible Story Crafts* by Melissa Rossetti Folini. Santa Barbara, CA: Libraries Unlimited. Copyright © 2010.

NOTES

SPIDERS

$\mathcal{S}$piders may not be as cute as ladybugs, but using some well-worded picture books, they can appear friendly and are not quite so scary. The children get to create a spider of their own to eat after the stories. You will be using many of the same ingredients for the spiders that you used for the ladybugs. This is a program you could do around Halloween as well.

Suggested Titles

Diary of a Spider by Doreen Cronin. HarperCollins, 2005. ISBN 0060001534.

The Itsy Bitsy Spider by Iza Trapani. Whispering Coyote, 1993. ISBN 1879085771.

Miss Spider's Tea Party by David Kirk. Scholastic, 1994. ISBN 0590477242.

Sophie's Masterpiece by Eileen Spinelli. Simon &Schuster, 2004. ISBN 0689866801.

The Very Busy Spider by Eric Carle. Putnam, 1984. ISBN 0399229191.

Edible Spider

Insects and Other Animals

Edible Spiders

Ingredients/Materials:

Round chocolate cream-filled cookies, enough for 1 per child

1 15-ounce tub of chocolate icing

Licorice "whips" cut into 1½-inch pieces, 8 per cookie

Plastic knives

Cocktail napkins/dessert plates

Plastic cups

Instructions:

- Give each child 1 cookie on a napkin/plate and a plastic knife.

- Have them frost the top and sides of the cookie with the icing.

- Then give them 8 licorice pieces each; they will insert 4 on one side and 4 on the opposite side, inserting them through the frosting and into the cream center of the cookie, for the spider's "legs."

NOTES

WOMBATS

*W*ombats are interesting little creatures from Australia that many children may not have previously heard about. In this activity the children do not actually make a wombat, but rather a fun version of "wombat stew," which goes with one of the stories they will have just heard.

Suggested Titles

Found You, Little Wombat by Angela McAllister. Sterling, 2003. ISBN 1402707088.

Sometimes I Like to Curl up in a Ball by Vicki Churchill. Sterling, 2001. ISBN 0806979437.

Swim, Little Wombat, Swim! by Charles Fuge. Sterling, 2005. ISBN 140272375.

Wombat Stew by Marcia K. Vaughan. Scholastic, 2008. ISBN 9781865046617.

Wombat Stew

Insects and Other Animals

Wombat Stew

Ingredients/Materials:

    1 12-ounce bag of chocolate chips (mud)
    1 15-ounce box of raisins (flies)
    1 7-ounce bag of coconut (feathers)
    1 8-ounce package of rainbow colored fruit candy (gum nuts)
    1 9-ounce package of gummy worms (slugs and bugs)
    Plastic cups or Styrofoam bowls
    Plastic spoons
    Cupcake liners
    Cardstock for labels (optional)

Wombat Stew Supplies

Instructions:

- Prior to story time, divide all the ingredients among the bowls or cups.

- *Optional:* Make labels out of the card stock and put one in front of each container indicating what it is (flies, feathers, etc.).

- Give each child a plastic spoon and a cupcake liner or plastic cup.

- Have the children go down the line, taking some ingredients from each container, until they have made their "stew." (This is actually more like a trail mix.)

- *Optional:* If you don't mind the mess and have more preparation time, substitute chocolate pudding for the chocolate chips and have a juicer "mud" to mix the other items into!

NOTES

BUTTERFLIES

*B*utterflies are some of the most graceful and well-loved residents of the insect world. Their metamorphosis from caterpillar to beautiful butterfly lends itself to wonderful discussions about not judging books by their covers or people by their outward appearance. They also present a fun science lesson about the stages of their metamorphosis. The books listed for this program cover all aspects of those beloved butterflies, and children will enjoy making a simple, edible butterfly at the end of the program.

This story time craft may be adapted to fit a program on dragonflies as well. Just change one ingredient in the craft. Suggested titles for that program are included here.

Suggested Titles

Butterflies

Butterfly House by Eve Bunting. Scholastic Press, 1999. ISBN 0590848844.

Clara Caterpillar by Pamela Duncan Edwards. HarperCollins, 2001. ISBN 0060289953.

I Wish I Were a Butterfly by James Howe. Gulliver Books, 1987. ISBN 0152380132.

Velma Gratch and the Way Cool Butterfly by Alan Madison. Schwartz & Wade, 2007. ISBN 0375835970.

Dragonflies

Are You a Dragonfly? by Judy Allen. Kingfisher, 2004. ISBN 0753458055.

Eliza and the Dragonfly by Susie Caldwell Rinehart. Dawn Publications, 2004. ISBN 1584690593.

Izzy the Dizzy Dragonfly by Teri Grule. Tate Publishing, 2009. ISBN 1606966898.

Edible Butterflies

Insects and Other Animals

Edible Butterfly

Ingredients/Materials:

> Mini pretzel twists, 2 per child
>
> Mini Tootsie Roll™ candies, 1 per child
>
> Cocktail napkins/dessert plates
>
> Tubes of black gel or cups of chocolate icing and plastic knives (optional)

Instructions:

- Give each child 2 pretzel twists and 1 candy on a napkin or plate.

- Have the children unwrap the candy by rolling it gently in between their hands for about 5 seconds to soften it. They should make sure to keep the shape.

- Then have the children take 1 pretzel twist and gently push the bottom or pointed end into the side of the softened candy; repeat on the other side. Caution them not to push too hard because the pretzel will break. It would be wise to keep some extra pretzels nearby.

- If the candy is simply too hard, give each child a plastic knife and a dollop of chocolate icing to dab on each side and then insert the pretzels into the icing.

Adapting the program for dragonflies:

- Use regular-sized tootsie roll candy (not the mini version).

- Have the children "warm up" the top third of the candy in their hands, then insert the pretzels twist in the top third, leaving more candy length to make the dragonfly's "tail."

From *Story Times Good Enough to Eat!: Thematic Programs with Edible Story Crafts* by Melissa Rossetti Folini. Santa Barbara, CA: Libraries Unlimited. Copyright © 2010.

NOTES

Chapter 6

Miscellaneous Themes

*T*his low-maintenance program includes entertaining stories about fairies; for a snack the children are simply given "pixie" sticks. As these are pure sugar, encourage the children to take them home to eat at their parents' discretion. Weather permitting, you may have the children make the "fairy houses" discussed in one of the books after this program. To do this, ask the children to bring some little nature- and earth-friendly items to the program, such as sticks, rocks, shells, and flowers. After the program, move to an area outside, where they can create a little home for their fairy friends.

Suggested Titles

Fairy Flight by Tracy Kane. Light Beams, 2003. ISBN 0970810423.

Fairy Houses by Tracy Kane. Light Beams, 2001. ISBN 0970810458.

Good Night, Fairies by Kathleen Hague. Sea Star Books, 2002. ISBN 1587171341.

The Knot Fairy by Bobbie Hinman. Best Fairy Books, 2007. ISBN 0978679101.

Pixy Stix

Pixie Sticks

Ingredients/Materials:

Small Pixy Stix™, 1 per child

10- to 12-inch lengths of colored curling ribbon, 1 per child (optional)

Scissors and plastic knives (for use by adults) (optional)

Instructions:

- When the stories are finished (and after you have built your fairy houses), give each child a Pixy Stix "wand" to take home.

- *Optional:* Make wands by having the children tie the curling ribbon around the sticks. This helps ensure the sticks remain unopened at least until the children leave. Have an adult help the children "curl" the ribbon with scissors or plastic knives. They can even be curled by putting the ribbon between 2 fingers and "scraping" the nails down the ribbon streamer.

- *Note:* Remind the children that the ribbon and the paper wrapping on the Pixy Stix are not edible.

NOTES

GRADUATION

*T*here are many types of graduations held throughout the year. Use this program when your children are graduating from one grade to the next, or at the time of year when local schools and colleges are having commencements.

Suggested Titles

Biscuit's Graduation Day by Alyssa Satin Capucilli. HarperFestival, 2005. ISBN 00600094656.

Happy Graduation by Namrata Tripathi. HarperFestival, 2003. ISBN 0060010096. A board book with a sing-a-long musical button. For your very young readers.

Miss Bindergarten Celebrates the Last Day of Kindergarten by Joseph Slate. Puffin, 2008. ISBN 0142410608.

Edible Diploma

Edible Diplomas

Ingredients/Materials:

White flour tortillas, enough for 1 per child (large ones may be cut in half)

1 pound package of deli ham slices

Individually wrapped 1-ounce cheese slices, enough for 1 per child

Ribbon or string cut into 6- to 8-inch pieces, 1 per child

Mayonnaise or mustard (optional)

Dessert plates

Plastic knives (optional)

Instructions:

- Give each child a plate and a tortilla.

- Instruct the children to spread on the mayo or mustard with the plastic knives (if using them).

- The children then take 1 or 2 slices of ham and lay it in the center of the tortilla.

- Then they take a piece of cheese and lay it in the center of the ham.

- Have them roll up their tortillas, into a long cylinder shape.

- Give each child a piece of string or ribbon to "tie" around the diplomas. They can then eat them!

- *Optional:* Use peanut butter and jelly for the filling. This spreads very well and helps hold the diploma together. Make sure to check for nut allergies first.

- *Note:* Caution the children that the ribbon and string are not edible.

From *Story Times Good Enough to Eat!: Thematic Programs with Edible Story Crafts*
by Melissa Rossetti Folini. Santa Barbara, CA: Libraries Unlimited. Copyright © 2010.

NOTES

$\mathcal{M}$any people love the ocean, and there are many ways to introduce it to children. You can focus on the water, things to do at the beach, or the things that dwell beneath the surface. Several titles in <u>The Rainbow Fish</u> series have wonderful lessons hidden in them that you could use in a program.

Following the stories children will have a chance to make and eat the "whole ocean!"

Suggested Titles

Hello Ocean by Pam Muñoz Ryan. Charlesbridge Publishing, 2001. ISBN 0881069884.

Out of the Ocean by Debra Frasier. Harcourt, Brace, Jovanovich, 1998. ISBN 015216349.

The Rainbow Fish by Marcus Pfsiter. North-South Books, 1992. ISBN 1558580107.

Stella, Star of the Sea by Mary-Louise Gay. Groundwood Books, 1990. ISBN 0888993374.

Way Down Deep in the Deep Blue Sea by Jan Peck. Simon & Schuster Children's Publishing, 2004. ISBN 0689851103.

Gelatin Ocean

Miscellaneous Themes

Gelatin Ocean

Ingredients/Materials:

1 3-ounce box of blue raspberry gelatin per 5–6 oceans, prepared according to the package directions

Red gummy fish, enough for 2–3 per child

Plastic cups

Plastic spoons

Gelatin Ocean Supplies

Instructions:

- Prior to story time, divide the gelatin into individual plastic cups.

- Give each child 1 cup of the "ocean" and a plastic spoon.

- Give the children each 2–3 gummy fish and have them insert them into the gelatin. They can do this by using the handle end of the spoon and making holes in the gelatin.

- *Optional:* If you are short on time and supplies, an alternative craft is to have the children fill snack-sized plastic bags with just the gummy fish or assorted fish-shaped crackers. They can then take their fish friends "to go."

Alternative Snack

*T*he old standby sandwich, peanut butter and jelly, gets its own program, celebrating the wonder of one of the world's favorite lunchtime staples. **Obviously you will need to check for any nut allergies before serving this craft.** You might also make jam sandwiches if you find that peanut butter or any other "butter" substitutes just aren't feasible.

Suggested Titles

Carla's Sandwich by Debbie Herman. Flashlight Press, 2004. ISBN 0972922520.

The Giant Jam Sandwich by John Vernon Lord and Janet Burroway. Sandpiper Press, 1987. ISBN 0395442370.

Peanut Butter and Jelly: A Play Rhyme by Nadine Bernard Westcott. Puffin, 1992. ISBN 01450548521.

Peanut Butter and Jelly Sandwich

Peanut Butter and Jelly Sandwich

Ingredients/Materials:

White bread (2 slices per child)

1 28-ounce jar of creamy peanut butter

1 32-ounce jar of jelly, your choice of flavor

Plastic knives

Cocktail napkins

Plastic cups

Child-friendly plastic cookie cutters in assorted shapes (optional)

Instructions:

- Give each child 2 slices of bread on a cocktail napkin and a plastic knife.

- Have the children put jelly on one slice of bread and peanut butter on the other.

- They may then choose which way they want to cut their sandwiches, diagonally or straight down the middle.

- *Optional:* If you are using the cookie cutters, the children may cut their sandwiches into fun shapes. For instance, if it is fall you could use pumpkin- or leaf-shaped cookie cutters.

- When they're done, serve the sandwiches with a glass of milk!

From *Story Times Good Enough to Eat!: Thematic Programs with Edible Story Crafts* by Melissa Rossetti Folini. Santa Barbara, CA: Libraries Unlimited. Copyright © 2010.

NOTES

WIZARDS AND MAGIC

*W*izards, witches, and all things magical have become extremely popular and less taboo over the last several years, and these themes can make for very fun programs. These books show the lighter side of magic, and at the end the children will get to make their very own edible magic wands!

I have also included a recipe for a witch's "selection" hat, which you could use with a Halloween program (see chapter 1).

Suggested Titles

The Last of the Wizards by Rona Jaffe. Golden Books, 2001. ISBN 0307106195.

The Magic Hat by Mem Fox. Harcourt, Brace, Jovanovich, 2002. ISBN 0152010254.

The War of the Wizards: A Magical Hologram Book by Stephen Wylie. Dial Books, 1994. ISBN 0803716907.

The Wizard by Jack Prelutsky. Greenwillow Books, 2008. ISBN 0061240761.

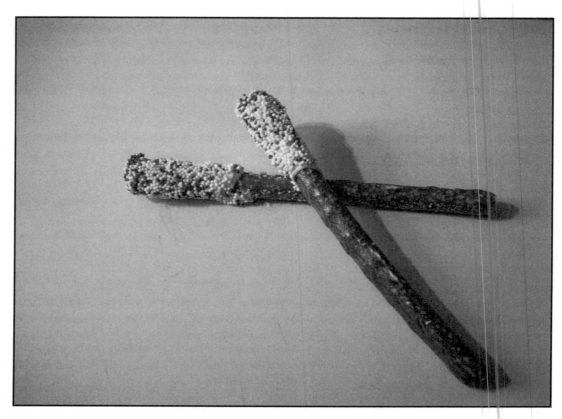

Edible Magic Wands

Edible Magic Wands

Ingredients/Materials:

Pretzel rods, 1 per child

1 15oz tub of white icing (tinted with food coloring if you wish)

Tubs of assorted colored sprinkles, jimmies, and nonpareils.

Plastic cups

Paper plates

Cocktail napkins

Instructions:

- If you choose to use a color other than white, tint the icing prior to story time (a few hours or a day ahead). Put the icing in paper cups. Also divide the assorted sprinkles, etc., onto paper plates.

- Give each child 1 full pretzel rod on a cocktail napkin.

- Have the children roll their pretzels in the icing, covering from the end to about one-quarter of the length of the rod.

- Then have them roll the frosted part of their pretzels in the jimmies, etc., on the paper plates. Presto, they've created their own magic wands!

Witch Hat

Miscellaneous Themes

Witch Hats

This craft may be used in addition to or instead of the wands. It's also good to use with a Halloween program.

Ingredients/Materials:

Round fudge-striped shortbread cookies, 1 per child

1 15-ounce tub of chocolate icing

Chocolate kisses (unwrapped), 1 per child

Plastic knives

Cocktail napkins/dessert plates

Plastic cups

Instructions:

- Give each child 1 cookie on a napkin/plate and a plastic knife.

- Tell the children to turn their cookies upside down and frost the entire bottom.

- Then give each child a chocolate kiss to place point side up in the center of the cookie. Now they have yummy chocolate hats!

NOTES

PLAYING DRESS UP

*L*ittle children love to pretend. They spend hours making up stories and characters, pretending that they are princesses, knights, cowboys, and just grown-ups in general. This program explores the make-believe with manners, parties, and a dress-up theme. It is geared mainly toward little girls and may also be hosted as a pajama time story time or a special "mommy and me" program. Encourage children to bring some borrowed dress-up items to the program such as gloves or feather boas, or have the mothers and daughters both attend wearing hats!

Suggested Titles

Fancy Nancy by Jane O'Connor. HarperCollins, 2005. ISBN 0060542098.

Fancy Nancy's Fashion Parade by Jane O'Connor. HarperFestival, 2008. ISBN 0061236012

Maisy Dresses Up by Lucy Cousins. San Val, 1999. ISBN 061321952X. This book is excellent for very young children.

Pinkalicious by Victoria Kann. HarperCollins, 2006. ISBN 0060776390.

Tea for Ruby by Sara Ferguson, the Duchess of York. Simon & Schuster, 2008. ISBN 1416954198.

Edible Necklace

Miscellaneous Themes

Edible Necklace and Bracelet

Ingredients/Materials:

1 14-ounce box of multicolored round cereal with holes

String, ribbon, or cord (cut into 25- to 30-inch lengths), 1 per child

String, ribbon, or cord (cut into 8- to 10-inch lengths), 1 per child

Styrofoam or plastic bowls

Instructions:

• Fill several bowls with the dry cereal, 1 bowl for every 4–5 children. Place the bowls in the middle of your craft area.

• Give each child 2 pieces of string (one of each length).

• Instruct the children to slide 20 or so pieces of cereal onto the longer string to form their necklaces. Help them tie a knot in the end.

• Have them do the same with the shorter piece of string to form their bracelets, using 10-12 pieces of cereal. Help them tie a knot in the end.

• They now have a matching set of edible jewelry to wear, then eat.

• *Note:* Please caution the children to eat the cereal only and not the string.

NOTES

Chapter 7

Easy Nonfood Theme Programs

   This chapter focuses on a few popular themes and very easy programs with simple crafts that can be done with little expense and preparation. These are not edible crafts but are simply a few suggestions for programs on some well-known themes that use similar materials, and they will still save you time and money!

FOURTH OF JULY

*I*ndependence Day is a fun day filled with parades and fireworks; and this program conveys the fun in a few unique books with a nice giveaway at the end. This is a great night or pajama time program, as it does not include a sugary snack right before bedtime; however, doing this at night makes the giveaway much more "noticeable."

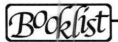

Suggested Titles

Beacon the Bright Little Firefly by Joe Troiano. Holiday Hill Farm, 2002. ISBN 0760732108.

Fourth of July Mice by Betty Roberts. Clarion Books, 2001. ISBN 0618313664.

Happy 4th of July, Jenny Sweeny by Leslie Kimmelman. Albert Whitman, 2007. ISBN 0807531529.

Hats Off for the 4th of July by Harriet Ziefert. Viking, 2000. ISBN 0670891185.

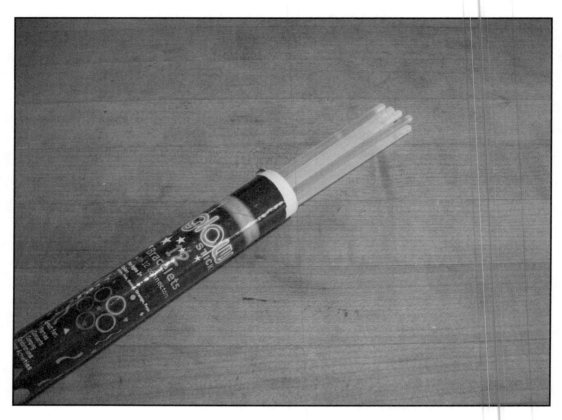

Glow Sticks

Easy Nonfood Theme Programs

Glow Sticks

Ingredients/Materials:

1 tube or several small packages of glow sticks, necklaces, or bracelets, 1 per child (sold at discount, dollar, and party stores in many lengths and package sizes)

Instructions:

- After the story time program is over, dim the lights and "crack" the sticks to activate them, then hand them out, giving 1 to each child. These are always a HUGE hit.

Additional program ideas if time permits:

- Have the children sing "Happy Birthday" to America.

- Hand out sheets of white copy paper folded in half lengthwise and some crayons or markers. Have children make greeting cards for "America's Birthday." They may draw what they love most about their country or pictures of fireworks. Hang up the cards in your area or let the children take them home to display there.

NOTES

OLYMPICS (SUMMER OR WINTER)

*T*he Olympics always bring a great deal of fanfare and patriotism with them; for those two weeks, many Americans are glued to our television sets. It's difficult not to want to participate. This program lets the children in on some of the sports and history behind the games, and shows them some other aspects of the Olympics as well. There is a book that teaches them about the Special Olympics as well as a book written by an Olympic athlete with a positive message for sports and for life. When they are done listening to the stories, the children will make their very own Olympic torches!

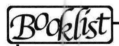

Suggested Titles

Elympics (poems) by X. J. Kennedy. Philomel, 1999. ISBN 0399232494.

Olympics by B. G. Hennessy and Michael Chesworth. Puffin, 1996. ISBN 0140384871.

A Very Special Athlete by Dale Bachman Flynn. Pearl Press, 2004. ISBN 0974133213.

Winners Never Quit by Mia Hamm. HarperCollins, 2006. ISBN 0060740507.

Olympic Torch

Easy Nonfood Theme Programs

Olympic Torch

Ingredients/Materials:

Flat-bottomed ice cream cones, 1 per child

Silver spray paint

Several sheets of orange-colored tissue paper cut into quarters, 1 for each child

Glue (white, nontoxic) (Glue sticks will not work very well with this craft.)

Plastic cups

Popsicle sticks

Instructions:

- Prior to story time (a few hours or a day ahead), spray paint all the cones with the silver paint. One large can should be enough to cover all of them.

- Give 1 cone to each child and explain that they have been painted and therefore cannot be eaten.

- Give each child a popsicle stick and a square of tissue paper.

- Have the children place a few drops of glue in the bottom and on the lower sides on the inside of the cone.

- Then have them fold the tissue paper into a triangle, bring the two bottom points of the triangle together, and set it into the cone. Now they have their very own, safe "eternal flames."

From *Story Times Good Enough to Eat!: Thematic Programs with Edible Story Crafts* by Melissa Rossetti Folini. Santa Barbara, CA: Libraries Unlimited. Copyright © 2010.

NOTES

STATUE OF LIBERTY

*T*he Statue of Liberty is one the most well-known and recogniz-able American symbols. This program celebrates and ex-plains the story behind lady liberty and lets the children make torches of their own. This is a very easy, low-maintenance program, because it uses the same materials as the Olympic torch. You may choose to use silver tissue to make a silver flame instead of the or-ange "fire" of the Olympic torch.

Suggested Titles

How the Second Grade Got $8,205.50 to Visit the Statue of Liberty by Nathan Zimelman and Bill Slavin. Albert Whitman, 1992. ISBN 0807534315.

L Is for Liberty by Wendy Cheyette Lewison. Grosset & Dunlap, 2003. ISBN 0448432285.

Liberty! by Allan Drummond. Farrar, Straus & Giroux, 2002. ISBN 0374343853.

Liberty's Journey by Kelly Dipucchio. Hyperion, 2004. ISBN 0786856262.

Liberty's Torch

Easy Nonfood Theme Programs

Liberty's Torch

Ingredients/Materials:

Flat-bottomed ice cream cones, 1 per child

Silver spray paint

Several sheets of orange- and/or silver-colored tissue paper cut into quarters, 1 for each child

Glue (white, nontoxic) (Glue sticks will not work very well with this craft.)

Plastic cups

Popsicle sticks

Instructions:

- Prior to story time (a few hours or a day ahead), spray paint all the cones with the silver paint. One large can should be enough to cover all of them.

- Give 1 cone to each child and explain that they have been painted and therefore cannot be eaten.

- Give each child a popsicle stick and a square of tissue paper.

- Have the children place a few drops of glue in the bottom and on the lower sides on the inside of the cone.

- Then have them fold the tissue paper into a triangle, bring the two bottom points of the triangle together, and set it into the cone.

NOTES

Index

About the Author

MELISSA ROSSETTI FOLINI is a full-time writer and retired director of the Chester Public Library in Chester, New Hampshire. She has published several short stories and poems, and for several years wrote a monthly book column in the *Derry News* newspaper. She has also owned a restaurant, worked part-time for a professional hockey team, and worked as a Christmas elf. She lives in Chester with her husband, one cat, and their ravenous dog, Max.